FRANCIS FRITH'S

STROUD

PHOTOGRAPHIC MEMORIES

HOWARD BEARD was born in Stroud and educated at Marling School and Manchester University. He is married with two grown-up children. After almost four decades in teaching, he has just retired from a post at Beaudesert Park Preparatory School near Minchinhampton. A keen genealogist since his school days, Howard has also worked professionally as a family historian, mostly for foreign clients. An enthusiastic collector, especially of early postcards and topographical photographs, he has written several local history books and enjoys lecturing extensively around Gloucestershire. His other interests include travel, choral singing, the theatre and walking in the countryside.

FRANCIS FRITH'S
PHOTOGRAPHIC MEMORIES

STROUD

PHOTOGRAPHIC MEMORIES

HOWARD BEARD

First published in the United Kingdom in 2003 by
Frith Book Company Ltd

Limited Hardback Subscribers Edition Published in 2003
ISBN 1-85937-796-3

Paperback Edition 2003
ISBN 1-85937-538-3

British Library Cataloguing in Publication Data

Francis Frith's Stroud - Photographic Memories
Howard Beard
ISBN 1-85937-538-3

Frith Book Company Ltd
Frith's Barn, Teffont,
Salisbury, Wiltshire SP3 5QP
Tel: +44 (0) 1722 716 376
Email: info@francisfrith.co.uk
www.francisfrith.co.uk

Printed and bound in Great Britain

Front Cover: **STROUD**, *High Street 1910* 62676
Frontispiece: **STROUD**, *Cainscross 1925* 77565

*The colour-tinting is for illustrative purposes only, and is not intended
to be historically accurate*

Acknowledgements
The author extends his grateful thanks to Peter Griffin and
Lionel Walrond for proof-reading the text; also to his wife, Sylvia,
for her constant encouragement and assistance.

AS WITH ANY HISTORICAL DATABASE THE FRITH ARCHIVE IS
CONSTANTLY BEING CORRECTED AND IMPROVED AND THE
PUBLISHERS WOULD WELCOME INFORMATION ON OMISSIONS OR
INACCURACIES

CONTENTS

FRANCIS FRITH
VICTORIAN PIONEER

FRANCIS FRITH, founder of the world-famous photographic archive, was a complex and multi-talented man. A devout Quaker and a highly successful Victorian businessman, he was philosophic by nature and pioneering in outlook.

By 1855 he had already established a wholesale grocery business in Liverpool, and sold it for the astonishing sum of £200,000, which is the equivalent today of over £15,000,000. Now a very rich man, he was able to indulge his passion for travel. As a child he had pored over travel books written by early explorers, and his fancy and imagination had been stirred by family holidays to the sublime mountain regions of Wales and Scotland. 'What lands of spirit-stirring and enriching scenes and places!' he had written. He was to return to these scenes of grandeur in later years to 'recapture the thousands of vivid and tender memories', but with a different purpose. Now in his thirties, and captivated by the new science of photography, Frith set out on a series of pioneering journeys up the Nile and to the Near East that occupied him from 1856 until 1860.

INTRIGUE AND EXPLORATION

These far-flung journeys were packed with intrigue and adventure. In his life story, written when he was sixty-three, Frith tells of being held captive by bandits, and of fighting 'an awful midnight battle to the very point of surrender with a deadly pack of hungry, wild dogs'. Wearing flowing Arab costume, Frith arrived at Akaba by camel seventy years before Lawrence of Arabia, where he encountered 'desert princes and rival sheikhs, blazing with jewel-hilted swords'.

He was the first photographer to venture beyond the sixth cataract of the Nile. Africa was still the mysterious 'Dark Continent', and Stanley and Livingstone's historic meeting was a decade into the future. The conditions for picture taking confound belief. He laboured for hours in his wicker dark-room in the sweltering heat of the desert, while the volatile chemicals fizzed dangerously in their trays. Back in London he exhibited his photographs and was 'rapturously cheered' by members of the Royal Society. His reputation as a photographer was made overnight.

VENTURE OF A LIFE-TIME

Characteristically, Frith quickly spotted the opportunity to create a new business as a specialist publisher of photographs. He lived in an era of immense and sometimes violent change.

For the poor in the early part of Victoria's reign work was exhausting and the hours long, and people had precious little free time to enjoy themselves. Most had no transport other than a cart or gig at their disposal, and rarely travelled far beyond the boundaries of their own town or village. However, by the 1870s the railways had threaded their way across the country, and Bank Holidays and half-day Saturdays had been made obligatory by Act of Parliament. All of a sudden the working man and his family were able to enjoy days out and see a little more of the world.

With typical business acumen, Francis Frith foresaw that these new tourists would enjoy having souvenirs to commemorate their days out. In 1860 he married Mary Ann Rosling and set out on a new career: his aim was to photograph every city, town and village in Britain. For the next thirty years he travelled the country by train and by pony and trap, producing fine photographs of seaside resorts and beauty spots that were keenly bought by millions of Victorians. These prints were painstakingly pasted into family albums and pored over during the dark nights of winter, rekindling precious memories of summer excursions.

THE RISE OF FRITH & CO

Frith's studio was soon supplying retail shops all over the country. To meet the demand he gathered about him a small team of photographers, and published the work of independent artist-photographers of the calibre of Roger Fenton and Francis Bedford. In order to gain some understanding of the scale of Frith's business one only has to look at the catalogue issued by Frith & Co in 1886: it runs to some 670 pages, listing not only many thousands of views of the British Isles but also many photographs of most European countries, and China, Japan, the USA and Canada - note the sample page shown on page 9 from the hand-written Frith & Co ledgers recording the pictures. By 1890 Frith had created the greatest specialist photographic publishing company in the world, with over 2,000 sales outlets - more than the combined number that Boots and WH Smith have today! The picture on the next page shows the Frith & Co display board at Ingleton in the Yorkshire Dales (left of window). Beautifully constructed with a mahogany frame and gilt inserts, it could display up to a dozen local scenes.

POSTCARD BONANZA

The ever-popular holiday postcard we know today took many years to develop. In 1870 the Post Office issued the first plain cards, with a pre-printed stamp on one face. In 1894 they allowed other publishers' cards to be sent through the mail with an attached adhesive halfpenny stamp. Demand grew rapidly, and in 1895 a new size of postcard was permitted called the court card, but there was little room for illustration. In 1899, a year after Frith's death, a new card measuring 5.5 x 3.5 inches became the standard format, but it was not until 1902 that the divided back came into being, so that the address and message could be on one face and a full-size illustration on the other. Frith & Co were in the vanguard of postcard development: Frith's sons Eustace and Cyril continued their father's monumental task, expanding the number of views offered to the public and recording more and more places in Britain, as the

		St Catherine's College		+	+
6	•	Senate House & Library		+	
7	•				+
8	•	Garrard Hostel Bridge			+	+	+
30	•	Geological Museum		+	+
1	•	Addenbrooke's Hospital		+	
2	•	St Mary's Church		+	
3	•	Fitzwilliam Museum, Pitt Press &c		+	
4	•			+	
5	Buxton, The Crescent				+
6	•	The Colonnade			+
7	•	Public Gardens			+
8	•				+
9	•				+
40	Haddon Hall, View from the Terrace				+
	Miller's Dale				+

coasts and countryside were opened up to mass travel.

Francis Frith had died in 1898 at his villa in Cannes, his great project still growing. The archive he created continued in business for another seventy years. By 1970 it contained over a third of a million pictures showing 7,000 British towns and villages.

FRANCIS FRITH'S LEGACY

Frith's legacy to us today is of immense significance and value, for the magnificent archive of evocative photographs he created provides a unique record of change in the cities, towns and villages throughout Britain over a century and more. Frith and his fellow studio photographers revisited locations many times down the years to update their views, compiling for us an enthralling and colourful pageant of British life and character.

We are fortunate that Frith was dedicated to recording the minutiae of everyday life. For it is this sheer wealth of visual data, the painstaking chronicle of changes in dress, transport, street layouts, buildings, housing, engineering and landscape that captivates us so much today. His remarkable images offer us a powerful link with the past and with the lives of our ancestors.

THE VALUE OF THE ARCHIVE TODAY

Computers have now made it possible for Frith's many thousands of images to be accessed almost instantly. Frith's images are increasingly used as visual resources, by social historians, by researchers into genealogy and ancestry, by architects and town planners, and by teachers involved in local history projects.

In addition, the archive offers every one of us an opportunity to examine the places where we and our families have lived and worked down the years. Highly successful in Frith's own era, the archive is now, a century and more on, entering a new phase of popularity. Historians consider the Francis Frith Collection to be of prime national importance. It is the only archive of its kind remaining in private ownership. Francis Frith's archive is now housed in an historic timber barn in the beautiful village of Teffont in Wiltshire. Its founder would not recognize the archive office as it is today. In place of the many thousands of dusty boxes containing glass plate negatives and an all-pervading odour of photographic chemicals, there are now ranks of computer screens. He would be amazed to watch his images travelling round the world at unimaginable speeds through internet lines.

The archive's future is both bright and exciting. Francis Frith, with his unshakeable belief in making photographs available to the greatest number of people, would undoubtedly approve of what is being done today with his lifetime's work. His photographs depicting our shared past are now bringing pleasure and enlightenment to millions around the world a century and more after his death.

STROUD
AN INTRODUCTION

THE TOWN of Stroud lies at the convergence of five valleys in a south-western corner of the Cotswold Hills. The scarp on which it is built drains towards the Severn. Just a few miles to the east, at the summit of the Cotswolds, the Thames and its tributaries flow gently towards London. In hilly parts of the Stroud district, the creamy local limestone supplied the principal construction material, whereas villages in the Severn Valley, beyond reasonable carting distance from quarries, generally used brick, and before that timber, even in high status buildings. Small marine fossils are frequently found in many local rock strata, while in certain places, such as Cainscross gravel pit, much larger specimens, for instance mammoth tusks, have been unearthed. Evidence of the activities of prehistoric man is to be found in long and round barrows and in worked flints. Dating from a later period, the major earthworks on

STROUD, *Thrupp 1900* 45586

Painswick Beacon and Minchinhampton Common are impressive.

Many villas with mosaic floors bear witness to several centuries of peaceful Roman settlement in the district. The 66-room villa at Woodchester is particularly grand, with its fine, though damaged, Orpheus pavement. There are two villas at Frocester, one of which has, exceptionally, been excavated each season for forty years.

According to Sir Robert Atkyns, Stroud takes its name from the Saxon 'strogd', which means 'scattered', and refers to its houses lying dispersed at a distance from each other. However, A H Smith's *The Place Names of Gloucestershire* suggests an alternative derivation from 'strod', meaning 'marshy land overgrown with brushwood'. The town is not even mentioned in the *Domesday Book*, since it was at that period merely an outlying part of Bisley Parish.

By 1304 Stroud had acquired independent parochial status, the 700th anniversary of which will be celebrated in 2004 with a variety of events, displays and activities.

From the Middle Ages, and indeed right through to the 20th century, Stroud has been known for its connection with the woollen cloth trade. Names of manufacturers such as Marling and Evans or Strachan come readily to mind, Strachan and Co being famous for the cloth used on snooker and billiard tables, whilst William Playne and Co still produce felt for nearly 1.5 million tennis balls per week. That a prosperous town should have arisen at the meeting of several valleys, all supplying water power for a profusion of mills, is unsurprising, and by the early 1800s many owners were installing steam engines to increase their production capacity.

Transport of goods to and from the Stroud valleys was enhanced by the construction of two major canals, the Stroudwater, which opened in 1779, and its through link towards the east, the Thames and Severn, inaugurated ten years later. At the time of writing, full restoration of these waterways is beginning.

STROUD, *George Street c1955* S224024

Brunel's Great Western Railway arrived in the mid 1840s, further accelerating the speed with which Stroud's manufactured goods could be transported, and predictably sounding the death knell for economical water-borne freight. Carriage of goods by road had also become more practical with the setting up of turnpikes a generation or so earlier. Because of improvements in land drainage, roads were now able to follow the valley bottoms, superseding former hilltop routes.

The Reform Act of 1832 had seen Stroud and its surrounding villages constituted a Parliamentary Borough, returning two members. At the time of the Act it was felt that Stroud should acquire public buildings befitting its enhanced status. The Subscription Rooms opened in 1834, and Bedford Street Congregational Chapel, put up in 1837, was seen as complementing it, together with Libby's Cloth Hall opposite, completed in 1871. Stroud Union Workhouse, in Bisley Road, opened in 1837 and the nearby cemetery was established in 1856. At around the same time it became clear that the parish church was manifestly inadequate for the population it served, even allowing for part of the ancient parish having been hived off to form Holy Trinity in 1839. The rebuilt St Lawrence's held its first service in 1868.

Stroud's first pioneering newspapers were *The Monthly Observer*, which began publication in 1848, and its successor, *The Free Press*, which was launched two years later. *The Stroud Journal* first appeared in 1854, and for most of the ensuing century supported the Liberal cause. *The Stroud News*, with which it was to eventually amalgamate, was founded in 1867. Its allegiance lay with the Conservative Party.

Built just below Holy Trinity Church, Stroud Hospital opened its doors to admissions in the 1870s. By the end of the century, most of the public buildings familiar to Stroud's residents had been erected – the Free Library in Lansdown (1888), the Holloway Institute in Russell Street (1895) and the School of Science and Art in Lansdown (1900).

Apart from the town's two Anglican churches, several non-conformist places of worship

CHALFORD, *The Church 1900* 45588

existed. There were two Congregationalist meeting houses, the Old Chapel, founded in 1711, and Bedford Street Chapel. By 1910 the Baptists had separated into two congregations, the earliest of which, established in 1824, met in John Street, while a breakaway group removed to the former Unitarian chapel in Lansdown (later a cinema and a dance school). The Methodists met in their Wesleyan chapel in Castle Street, and there was a Primitive Methodist chapel, now the Cotswold Playhouse, in Parliament Street. The Brethren worshipped at Acre Street, in the building originally occupied by the Methodists. The Roman Catholic church at Beeches Green had been founded in 1859. A synagogue had also opened in Lansdown in 1899 to serve Stroud's Jewish community, many of whom were employed in the clothing industry.

Stroud Choral Society had its origin in the 1830s, while the town's main amateur dramatic society, the Cotswold Players, was formed just before the First World War.

During the early part of the Great War VAD (Volunteer Aid Detachment) hospitals were opened, such as those functioning at Stroud's Trinity Rooms, Chestnut Hill House at Nailsworth and Standish House.

Grammar school education in Stroud began effectively in 1887 with the foundation of Marling School. The High School for Girls followed in 1904. There were also several private schools, such as Miss Isacke's Stratford Abbey College, which occupied a building on the site where Tesco's store now stands.

Celebrated inhabitants of the Stroud district include Dick Whittington, who was Lord of the Manor during the Middle Ages, John Canton (1718-1770), a mathematician who calculated the latitude of the town, and the astronomer James Bradley, who is buried at Minchinhampton; also, from a much later period, the novelist and poet Laurie Lee, the Rev Wilbert Awdry, who created the famous *Thomas the Tank Engine* books, and the cricketer Jack Russell.

Among Stroud's more famous visitors were

BRIMSCOMBE CORNER, *1910* 62690

John Wesley, who preached in the Shambles, the evangelist George Whitefield, the actor Edmund Kean, who married at Stroud, and the actress Sarah Siddons. In 1756 James Wolfe, of Quebec fame, was in Stroud to control disturbances amongst local weavers. Last, but by no means least, George III came to Stroud in the summer of 1788. P H Fisher's *Notes and Recollections of Stroud* records an interesting footnote to this visit. 'His Majesty wore a blue coat with a scarlet collar, the Windsor uniform, and a cocked hat, with which he acknowledged the salutation of the people and, when he raised his hat for that purpose, a rent was visible under the arm of his Majesty's coat.'

Space precludes mention of festivities and events within the Stroud area, but one episode cannot be allowed to go unrecorded. In August 1807, during the war with France, among a number of recruiting officers based at Stroud were Lieutenants Benjamin Heazle and Joseph Delmont. Following an argument, the latter made a remark that offended Heazle, who challenged him to a duel. With some difficulty suitable pistols were obtained, the encounter took place in the Grange Fields and Delmont was gravely wounded. It was thought that Heazle shot prematurely, before the call to fire was made. Heazle, not surprisingly, fled. Delmont is buried in St Lawrence's churchyard, his death hastened, so the story goes, by disinfectant administered internally instead of on the wound.

Following the decline in Stroud's staple industry, the woollen cloth trade, which was famous for weaving the scarlet cloth for guards' uniforms, a huge number of varied businesses have, over the past century, both occupied the premises of former cloth mills and also sprung up in new buildings. Names such as Hoffman, Sperry, Redler, Cope-Chat, Erinoid, E A Chamberlain, Newman and Hender and Daniels are examples. The contribution of such firms, and many others, to the success of the local economy is recognised in displays at Stroud's excellent new Museum in the Park. In

BISLEY, *The Wells 1910* 62696

this context, mention should also be made of Edwin Beard Budding, who in 1830 adapted a machine for trimming the nap on cloth into the world's first lawnmower.

The photographs in this collection are arranged to follow a sequence. From such vantage points as Rodborough Fort the imaginary traveller is led into the town itself and on to Stratford Park. Then passing up the Chalford Valley, with a diversion over the Commons, the Nailsworth Valley is reached. Continuing along the broad expanse of the Stonehouse Valley, the route concludes with the Painswick and Slad Valleys.

STONEHOUSE, *Parish Church c1960* S265044

DISTANT VIEWS OF THE TOWN

Overlooked as it is from several nearby hilltops, distant views of Stroud have always been popular. Detailed 19th-century landscape engravings of the town exist, and the Museum in the Park has on display an important oil painting by Alfred Smith, looking towards the town from Rodborough Fort. The picture dates from 1848, and shows an early locomotive on the recently completed railway viaduct. Half a century on, nationally important photographers such as Francis Frith set up their tripods at the same spot, and so did a host of local photographers, both amateur and professional. A picture taken from the Grange Fields complements the Rodborough ones, since it reveals other areas of the town hidden from the Fort by the curve of the hill on which Stroud stands.It is also, perhaps, worth making the point that a century or more ago, the distant views of Stroud included here would have been rather more familiar to local people than they are today. Before the mass ownership of the motor car, walking and picnicking on the hills around Stroud was all the less well off inhabitants of the town could afford.

STROUD, *From Rodborough 1900* 45729

This picture shows the lower part of Stroud, and is a partner for No 45728 (page 17). By 1900 most of the town's architectural landmarks were already standing. Clearly visible are Hill Paul's clothing factory and the Subscription Rooms, together with several non-conformist chapels, although what makes the picture additionally interesting is how little of the surrounding countryside was built up at this period.

STROUD
From Rodborough 1900
45728

The left third of this photograph comprises the early core of the town. From Holy Trinity Church, Stroud's red brick Victorian terraces and villas lead off towards the cemetery on the right and the Union Workhouse above it, which was originally surrounded by eight acres of land. P H Fisher's *Notes and Recollections of Stroud*, published in 1871, states that 'the adult paupers are employed in cultivating the land and garden and in other needful labour.'

STROUD, *From above Butter Row 1890* 25151

Upper Stroud is in the distance, with Park Road below, still at this period containing only a few large private houses. But it is the mills and factory chimneys at Bowbridge, mostly now demolished, which make the photograph interesting. In 1890 the canal (in the foreground) still carried some traffic. 'Butterow', incidentally, is the more modern spelling of the village where the picture was taken.

STROUD
*From near Folly Lane
1910* 62671

Here, from the fields off
Folly Lane, Stroud may be
admired from a very
different vantage point.
Today the allotments on the
near side of Uplands School
have been replaced by
housing, as have parts of
Rodborough Fields in the
middle distance.
Rodborough Fort, on the
skyline, now masked by
trees, remains an
unmistakeable landmark.

THE TOWN AND STRATFORD PARK

Stroud developed organically, and therefore in a haphazard manner. Separate clusters of houses, mostly uphill from the church, were progressively linked, from the medieval period, by building development, until solid street frontages came into being. From the end of the 18th century, the arrival of the canals, together with a number of important new toll roads, encouraged the natural centre of the town to move further downhill. The erection of the Subscription Rooms and Bedford Street Chapel in the 1830s, later flanked by Libby's Cloth Hall, created – on three sides – a pleasing town square.

The arrival of the Great Western Railway in the 1840s accelerated the transport of building brick, although much had been made in Stroud previously. This is one of the factors which led to the development of shopping and residential streets, such as Gloucester Street, Russell Street, George Street, Lansdown and London Road.

At a later period, further urban expansion took place at Lightpill, Uplands and Cainscross Road. Rodborough was effectively linked to Stroud by building at Wallbridge and Bath Road. Although piecemeal development has taken place over the last century, it would nevertheless be true to say that the basic shape of the centre of Stroud has not changed fundamentally since 1900.

STROUD, *Lansdown and the School of Science 1900* 45734

Lansdown developed in the late 19th century as a fashionable extension to the town. In it stood the School of Science and Art, Stroud's Victorian public library, the Christian Science Church and, further east, the Liberal Hall and the Synagogue. Census returns indicate that Stroud's Jewish community, mainly linked to the clothing industry, was mostly located in this area.

STROUD
The School of Science 1900
45735

When this photograph was taken, the School of Science and Art, which for so many years housed Stroud Museum, was only a year old. It is interesting to note that the gutter head by the porch is dated 1899. However, it was some time before the builders' scaffolding was actually taken down. This was due to an error in the contract for the carvings, which were never fully completed. Amongst them are stone medallion portraits of celebrated scientists such as Faraday, authors such as Barry and a representation of a steam train.

STROUD, *Gloucester Street c1955* S224021

Gloucester Street is another of Stroud's largely brick-built Victorian developments. In 1910 shops here included Tuck's the confectioners, Harry Stone's eating rooms and Jesse Isacke's beer store. At the lower end of the street the former magistrates' court and police station may be glimpsed. The Greyhound Inn in the foreground has recently undergone a major refurbishment.

▼ **STROUD,** *Bank Gardens c1960* S224040

The gardens behind Bank House, situated in the lower High Street, were given to the town of Stroud in 1930 by Mr Ernest Winterbotham, and were intended as a quiet corner where shop workers could enjoy a lunch break. In recent years the gardens have also become, in hot weather, a favourite spot for youthful sunbathers. Sad to say, the sundial has suffered from vandalism.

► **STROUD**
*The Parish Church
1900* 45581

With the exception of its 14th-century tower and spire, St Lawrence's Church is a Victorian rebuild, made necessary when its predecessor became too small to serve Stroud's increasing population. The foundation stone of the enlarged building was laid on 6 November 1866, and the church was dedicated by the Bishop of Gloucester for public worship on 4 August 1868.

◀ **STROUD**
*The Parish Church
1910* 62674

Here we can see a portion
of the gardens of Bank
House in the days before
they became accessible to
the public. Note the
thatched summerhouse. A
photograph exists, taken
from the same position in
the 1870s, showing Mr W
Cheriton, a member of
the church choir,
balancing on one leg on
the very top of the spire,
during renovation work!

▶ **STROUD**
*The Church, the Nave
looking East 1890*
25156

The church exterior is of
Bisley stone, while that
used for the interior walls,
most of the pulpit and the
base of the font, comes
from Painswick.
The floor tiles are from
Herefordshire. A few early
monuments survive from
the former church, notably
a fine 17th-century
memorial commemorating
the Stephens family of
Lypiatt. There are several
good Victorian
stained-glass windows.

STROUD, *The Town Hall 1925* 77564

The Town Hall, or the Market House as it was formerly known, is first recorded in 1594. P H Fisher's *Notes and Recollections of Stroud* states that 'to the ground floor of the Market House butter women and dealers in poultry, fruit and vegetables from the country formerly resorted on market days to sell their various commodities.' Opposite the building, across the Shambles, are ancient folding tables, once used by butchers.

STROUD
*The Old Almshouses
1925* 77573

The almshouses in Church Street are surely one of Stroud's more serious architectural losses. Dating from the early 17th century, these fine Cotswold stone buildings were undergoing restoration when war was declared in 1939, so work was put on hold. With materials unavailable, a partial collapse, due to the weather, followed and demolition was inevitable.

STROUD, *High Street c1955* S224012

Beyond Smith's chemist's shop, on the left, and the entrance to the Shambles, is another Smith's: Alma House clothing store. This business, founded in the 19th century, was formerly Birch's, and by 1885 Monaghan's. In the distance is the headquarters building of Stroud Co-operative Society, opened in 1931. Behind the car, with its familiar DG Gloucestershire registration, is one of Stroud's surviving Victorian pillar-boxes.

STROUD
High Street 1910 62676

Here we are looking down the High Street, with Smith's chemist's shop – still at this period with only one large window – on the right. Below it is Withey's grocery store, long-established even in 1910. When the building changed hands a few years ago, a large number of early grocery orders was discovered in an attic.

STROUD
High Street c1950
S224020

Several well-known chain stores feature here, in the lower part of the High Street – now, of course, pedestrianised. Curry's later relocated to King Street before finally leaving the town. Timothy White's (centre) is now Bewise, and Milward's is a card shop. Some years ago developers wanted to demolish this building with its fine Venetian window. Local protest successfully thwarted its removal.

STROUD, *King Street 1900* 45733

This open area, known as King Street Parade, was the scene of many local events. Empire Day, Coronation and Agricultural Show carnivals assembled here, before processing off to Fromehall Park or Stratford Park. The large building on the left, with its flagpole, was the Victoria Rooms. Built in 1831, it was named after the then princess. Horse, and later motor, buses departed from this area.

STROUD
King Street 1910
62679

Partly obscured by the lamp post and a tree stands the Royal George Hotel (left), demolished in the 1930s. Near it waits Spratt's horse bus, which served the Stonehouse Valley. The statue (right) commemorates Stroud's late 19th-century MP, George Holloway, founder of the Mid Gloucestershire Mutual Benefit Society. The road in the foreground was lowered when the railway arrived in 1845.

STROUD, *King Street 1925* 77562

By the mid 1920s the Midland Bank building, beyond Lewis and Godfrey's drapery store, had replaced Sidney Park's shop. The Royal George Hotel had by now ceased business. Hepworth's clothing establishment now occupied its ground floor. The entrance to The Picture House, one of Stroud's early cinemas, adjoins Hepworth's.

▼ **STROUD,** *King Street c1955* S224025

By the 1950s, King Street Parade had largely taken on its familiar present-day appearance. Woolworth's, still not rebuilt, occupied the Victoria Rooms site, while the Royal George Hotel was now reconstructed in Art Deco style as Burton's tailoring business. The neo-Georgian building housing Lloyds Bank had been erected on the left, just across Rowcroft Retreat. Road signs and pedestrian crossings had also appeared.

► **STROUD**

King Street c1960 S224052

Stroud residents above a certain age will remember the policeman directing traffic at the Town Time. The latter consisted of an accurate timepiece by Robert Bragg, set to 'Railway Time' and sited in the arched alcove just visible behind the lady on the right. It is now in Stroud Library. Gardner's, the hatters, has a model of a hat displayed above its shop front (left). The firm was in business for over a century.

◀ **STROUD**
George Street 1910
62678

The Wilts and Dorset Bank on the left, now the Natwest, was almost new when the picture was taken. It had entrances in both George Street and Russell Street. On the far left is the Post Office Inn. Horwood's fancy goods shop is on the corner with Bedford Street (right). The street nameplate, of which several survive, is a peculiarity of Stroud. It was a marble off cut from the Art Memorial Company's tombstone works, cut, etched and infilled with paint.

▶ **STROUD**
George Street c1955
S224042

Beyond the Singer Sewing Machine shop is Collins' stationery business (right). In the 1920s and 30s Walter Collins printed a well-known series of sepia postcards of the town. In the far distance the façade of the Ritz Cinema, which burnt down on 23 June 1961, can be seen. It was estimated at the time that 120,000 gallons of water were used in attempting to extinguish the blaze. Above the cinema, designed in distinctive 1930s style, was a popular restaurant.

STROUD
George Street c1955
S224035

Behind the 'No Waiting' sign outside Clark's drapery shop (left), we can glimpse the attractive double curved windows of North's, the chemist. Gibson's, on the right, was another long-established drapery concern. Note the proliferation of sun blinds needed to protect window displays from bright light.

▶ STROUD
Russell Street c1955
S224022

Here we are reminded that before the building of the bus station in Merrywalks, buses waited at several locations in the town. By 1955 both Russell Street and George Street had become one way, as the road signs indicate. Walter Wells (left) sold clocks - one of which survives in the Union Street Schoolroom - and jewellery, hence the ring sign above his shop front. The writer's cousin, Sidney Pearce, two doors down, advertised his saddlery business in a similar way with a model of a horse's head mounted on the wall. Sims' clock, one of Stroud's architectural curiosities, is in the foreground. A trough formerly stood by it for the use of the horses pulling early buses.

◀ STROUD
The Town Centre c1965
S224090

The Trustee Savings Bank building, on the right, was formerly the office of Stroud's Conservative newspaper, the *Stroud News*. Its Liberal rival, the *Stroud Journal*, occupied the premises in Lansdown from which its joint successor now operates. The cinema on the left, which opened in 1913 as the Empire, was later rebuilt in 1935 as the Gaumont and was the Mecca Bingo Hall when it closed a few years ago. The property is currently being re-developed.

▲ **STROUD,** *Beeches Green 1910* 62673

Taken from the GWR station platform, this picture shows a scene very considerably changed. Apart from the Catholic church complex on the ridge to the left, virtually all the buildings seen here, including Badbrook Mill, have gone, mostly around 1960, when Merrywalks, left, was widened. The gardens, too, have been replaced by tarmac and a doctors' surgery.

◄ **STROUD**
The Memorial Gardens c1965 S224083

Sidney B Park was a successful businessman; in Edwardian days he owned two drapery shops in Stroud. However, on 26 October 1917 his only son, Herbert, was killed in France, and in 1927 the Park family gave land to create a public garden in his memory. Sidney and his wife, Ellen, are buried in Stroud Cemetery.

◀ **STROUD**
*Stratford Park,
the Lake c1965*
S224076

The Mansion dates from the late 17th century and has variously served as a private house, a school and as the headquarters of an Anglican order of monks, the Community of the Glorious Ascension. With galleries added on the left, and reduced in height by one storey, it now houses Stroud's new Museum in the Park, opened in 2001.

◀ **STROUD**
Trinity Church
1890 25158

Holy Trinity Church
was built when
Stroud Parish was
subdivided in the
1830s. At a later
stage its twin
turrets became
unsafe and were
removed. The
interesting façade
of the hospital
beyond was also
lost when the Peace
Wing was added
just after World War
I. William Cowle's
private observatory,
seen further to the
right, has also long
since disappeared.

▲ **STROUD**, *Stratford Park, the Children's Playground c1965* S224074

Set in open land, with mature oaks nearby, Stratford Park playground has always proved a
popular magnet for parents with young children, who now mostly travel there by car. Present-
day attractions at the nearby Leisure Centre, built in the early 1970s, are extensive and include
an indoor pool, a sports hall, trampolines, squash and badminton courts, a gym, a sauna, a
solarium and a steam room.

◀ **STROUD**
Stratford Park,
the Swimming Pool
1938 88637

Little changed today, the
pool at Stratford Park
was opened in 1937 and
has always been popular,
with youngsters in
particular, during the
summer months. Many
school children learned
to swim here, just as
previous generations
had in the local canals,
often by being thrown in
and encouraged to stay
afloat! The parabolic
diving board is of
architectural interest.

STROUD
*Stratford Park,
the Bowling Green
c1955* S224006

In the period before mass ownership of motor cars enabled people to broaden their leisure horizons, Stratford Park, with its bowls, tennis courts and putting green, was visited by hundreds of local people on fine, sunny days. Most would arrive by bus, cycle or on foot. Picnics were often eaten on the grass under the trees by the bandstand.

THE CHALFORD VALLEY

The Chalford Valley is arguably one of the more important of the five radiating out from Stroud, since it leads to the east and eventually to London. During the 19th century it also held all three major transport systems – road, rail and canal. The valley is particularly rich in mills, once producing woollen cloth and now mostly occupied by small businesses.

Before the building of the main road, access up the valley was by lanes that joined small hamlets built along the spring line, such as Butter Row, Bagpath and Quarhouse. Chalford, some four miles from Stroud, is a large village, extending from the valley floor up its northern flank into Chalford Hill, where the system of roadways is so complicated that even local people can sometimes become lost. Ascending the hillside, the gradient is so steep that the only means of access to many of Chalford's attractive cottages is a network of paths where once bread and groceries were delivered by pack donkeys. Beyond Baker's Mill, towards Sapperton Tunnel, only the abandoned Thames and Severn Canal follows the valley bottom, creating a habitat exceptionally rich in flora and fauna.

STROUD, *On the Canal 1900* 45738

By 1900, the Thames and Severn Canal, photographed here near Capel's Viaduct, was in decline. Commercial traffic through Sapperton Tunnel ended in 1912, and the canal was formally closed in 1933. An interesting contemporary description of the canal occurs in Thurston Temple's *The Flower of Gloucester*. The main Cheltenham to Swindon railway line is to the right, with Butter Row Hill in the distance.

STROUD, *On the Canal 1910* 62681

Taken from a position slightly further east, this tranquil photograph shows Arundel Mill. The building is recorded as passing in 1585 to one Richard Arundel, who died in 1601. In 1837 four power looms were installed in the mill. Soon after this picture was taken, all its main buildings were demolished, though the weir and some ancillary structures survive today.

STROUD
Bowbridge and Butter Row 1900 45739

The photographer stood in a field at Weyhouse, just off Bowbridge Lane, to take this picture. The site of Excelsior Works, in the foreground, is now a bus depot. Just to its right is the roofline of a row of houses, also now demolished, which formerly included a blacksmith's forge and Bowbridge post office. A comparison with the scene today shows that several properties in Butter Row have gone, including a double-gabled house and a few cottages away to the left.

STROUD, *Butter Row, the Old Pike House 1925* 77568

On the board above the toll house door are listed the charges for the passage of vehicles and animals through the gate that once stood here. For example, 'stage coaches, post chaises or sociable Berlins' cost 3d, droves of oxen or cows 3d per score and calves or hogs a halfpenny less. In the late 1960s the writer lived in a cottage almost next door to the toll house, at which time an extrovert Italian kept it as a general store. He could frequently be heard standing in the road outside rendering snatches of Verdi! Further down the hill, part of Butter Row Methodist Chapel, now a private house, is visible.

THRUPP
and Montserrat
1910 62682

The absence of trees can alter a landscape almost beyond recognition. Today the road from Butter Row to Rodborough Common is completely wooded on its lower side. The footpath which follows it has all but vanished, and so has the ascending track at the top right of the picture.

BRIMSCOMBE, *The Valley 1900* 45741

Butter Row School, in the foreground, stands detached some distance from the community it served. It closed more than a generation ago. Thrupp clings to the hillside on the left. The Chalford Valley, with former woollen cloth mills every few hundred yards along its length, extends through Brimscombe into the distance. Brimscombe Church, Walls Quarry and the hill leading to Burleigh are top right.

THRUPP

1900 45586

Apart from a few older stone cottages, most of Thrupp's houses consist of Victorian brick terraces put up as dwellings for workers at Griffin, Ham or Hope Mills. The chimney of Brimscombe Brewery is visible on the right of the village, with Brimscombe Court beyond. The writer attended Thrupp school, the gables of which peep over the trees on the upper left.

BRIMSCOMBE, *Walls Quarry 1901* 47363

On the left is the main London railway line and, still further to the left, the Thames and Severn Canal. The buildings on the hill are the upper part of Brimscombe village, with Walls Quarry and Burleigh to the right. With the exception of the nearer dwellings, all the houses we see here are of Cotswold stone.

BRIMSCOMBE CORNER *1910* 62690

Brimscombe Corner has altered substantially. The road has been widened, and a row of shops, off camera to the left, demolished. The 18th-century hump-back bridge over the canal has also been removed. The Ship Inn survives, although the traditional, triple-gabled Cotswold house, centre right, has gone. The church and a row of weavers' cottages are visible in the distance.

BRIMSCOMBE, *The Valley 1900* 45590

This picture should more properly be captioned 'The Bourne from Besbury.' In the foreground lies Wimberley Mill, run in 1900 by the Critchley family as a pin factory. Hidden beyond it is the Thames and Severn Canal, and then the railway. Behind the viaduct on the left is Bourne Mill, formerly used by H S Hack to produce walking sticks. Brimscombe Port is in the distance.

▼ **BUSSAGE,** *The Vale 1910* 62702

The road we see here leads up the Toadsmoor Valley to Eastcombe, Bussage, and eventually Bisley. Beyond the first houses can be glimpsed the junction with Bourne Lane, on the far side of which today is a disused shop and S T B Engineering. Building work has recently taken place at the bottom left corner of the picture.

▶ **BUSSAGE**
Valley, Toadsmoor Lake 1910 62701

The lake at Toadsmoor is one of the prettiest spots in the district. Most pictures of it show the woodsman's cottage, half hidden among the trees. Back in January 1908 a prolonged and heavy frost led to literally thousands of local people flocking to Toadsmoor to skate. Two girls nearly drowned when the ice broke.

◀ **BUSSAGE**
The Church 1910
62698

Bussage is one of several parishes created in the 19th century by subdividing the extensive ancient parish of Bisley; as we saw earlier, until 1304 even Stroud itself was a chapelry within this parish. Old Bussage, in its hilltop position, is an attractive village. Its population has in recent years been considerably boosted by a large housing development.

▶ **CHALFORD**
The Golden Valley 1910 62709

This viewpoint on Coppice Hill is a favourite spot for photographing Chalford. The paths on the right of the picture are those along which bread delivery was made by panniered donkey. On the left is Chalford Station and, just below it, the Thames and Severn Canal.

CHALFORD
On the Canal 1910
62711

When this picture was taken, the canal had only recently undergone a restoration programme. Of the two pubs shown here, The New Red Lion (centre) survives. The Bell Inn (left) is now a private house. The retaining wall on the right was part of Chalford Station yard. The careful posing of the children adds considerably to the appeal of the photograph.

CHALFORD
The Vale 1890 25167

The viaduct on the left carries
the railway as it descends
from Sapperton Tunnel. Part
of Chalford Baptist Tabernacle
is on the right. In the distance
is Rack Hill, which acquired its
name from the racks on which
cloth was pegged out to dry.

MINCHINHAMPTON, AMBERLEY AND RODBOROUGH

Most of the towns and villages depicted in this collection of photographs are situated in one or other of the five valleys that meet at Stroud. Minchinhampton, however, is not, being built almost wholly on a high plateau of land midway between Chalford and Nailsworth.

The parish is an ancient one, including – until the 19th century – Brimscombe, Amberley and parts of Nailsworth such as Watledge. Its importance as a centre of the woollen cloth industry ensured Minchinhampton's prosperity, evidenced by a well-preserved late 17th-century Market House. The subsequent decline in the cloth trade, exacerbated by the railways bypassing the town, meant that little or no industrial development took place there. In consequence, Minchinhampton has retained an attractive atmosphere of unspoilt tranquillity.

Amberley, a mile or so away across the Common, has always been considered a desirable village in which to live. Under its pseudonym, Enderley, it was praised in Mrs Craik's *John Halifax, Gentleman*:

'Such a fresh, free, breezy spot;

How the wind sweeps over it.

I can feel it on my face still.'

Leaving Minchinhampton Common, we reach The Bear Inn, beyond which is a second great stretch of National Trust land, Rodborough Common. From here there are spectacular views across the River Severn into Wales.

MINCHINHAMPTON, *The View from Forwood c1955* M83045

The large house (middle right) is called The Shard. To its left, Well Hill ascends into Minchinhampton, with its curiously truncated church spire. According to two manuscript histories in the Bodleian Library, the upper part was blown off in a storm in 1602. The attractive cottages of King Street are on the left, with The Lammas beyond.

MINCHINHAMPTON
Below Well Hill 1901
47355

The battlement-like walls on the left belong to Lammas Park. The Lammas, built on higher ground away to the left, was once owned by the Sheppard family, who built nearby Gatcombe Park, now the home of the Princess Royal. The Lammas was formerly the Manor House of Minchinhampton.

MINCHINHAMPTON, *The Church Interior 1901* 47352

The inside of the church looks rather different today. The nave walls have been plastered and whitewashed and the chancel ceiling embellished. Most obviously, a rood screen, erected in memory of Harold Woollcombe-Boyce, who died on active service during the Great War, now spans the chancel arch.

53

MINCHINHAMPTON, *The Church, the Rose Window 1901* 47353

The south transept is a survival from the medieval church, which was so drastically altered during the 19th century. The tracery of the rose window is of an intricate design, and its Victorian glass is especially attractive when seen, lit from within, from the market square on winter evenings. The arched tombs beneath the window date from the 14th century.

MINCHINHAMPTON
*Gold Links, 3rd hole
1910* 62692

Golf has been played on Minchinhampton Common since at least 1889. The green shown here is just above Amberley village, not far from where the war memorial now stands. Today hawthorn bushes and other small trees obscure this view.

AMBERLEY, *Rose Cottage 1925* 77583

This attractive cottage, with its Gothic window frames, is situated close to Minchinhampton Common, although it is much less easy to see this today, since trees now cover the horizon. The cottage is celebrated as the house where Mrs Craik wrote *John Halifax, Gentleman* in 1856.

► **AMBERLEY**
Littleworth 1901
47356

This area of the village, photographed from just below the Amberley Inn, is substantially the same today, although the ruined cottage (centre left) has gone; to the left of it, a house constructed of corrugated iron now stands. A larger building, Highstones, presently occupies the space behind the pole on the right.

◄**RODBOROUGH**
The Golf Links 1910
62683

In the early part of the last century, the adjoining commons at Rodborough and Minchinhampton both had golf courses. Only the Minchinhampton Club survives today, though the contours of one of the Rodborough greens, shown here, remain clearly visible. The Bear Inn is on the left, with the hamlet of Houndscroft in the centre of the picture.

▲ **RODBOROUGH COMMON,** *The Bear Hotel 1925* 77575

Taken from a position a little further along the hillside from No 62683, this photograph shows the Bear Inn soon after its extension was completed. Just visible on the left is the roof of Beech Cottage, by 1927 owned by Sidney Howard Smith. The writer's aunt was for some years resident in Beech Cottage as Smith's cook-housekeeper.

◀ **RODBOROUGH**
The Bear Hotel 1910
62687

The Bear is recorded as a public house and stagecoach inn as early as 1751, positioned along the then route from Stroud via Minchinhampton to Cirencester. The long, striped building to the left was formerly the headquarters of the Stroud Golf Club, which played on the 9-hole Rodborough Common Course.

◄**RODBOROUGH**
The Fort 1890 25162A

On the slopes below the Fort, known in Edwardian times as Fort St George and run as a guest house and tearoom, the depressions in the hillside are largely the result of surface quarrying. Pictures of the Fort are dateable by reference to the pine trees that now front it, entirely absent in this early view.

◄ **RODBOROUGH**
*The Bear Hotel
1901* 47360

A comparison with the Bear Inn as it is today shows that the original double-gabled Cotswold stone structure has survived and been incorporated within the present building, the lowest floor now serving as the bar area.

▲ **RODBOROUGH,** *The Fort c1960* R311082

Some seventy years after No 25162A was taken, interesting changes have occurred. Pine trees now almost obscure the Fort. The cottage below it, which enjoys spectacular views, has acquired a sun lounge with a balcony and a dormer window, but has lost a chimney. Cattle graze Rodborough Common, which is now, as the sign indicates, owned by the National Trust.

◄ **RODBOROUGH**
The Village c1960
R311006

The access to Butter Row Lane has now been improved by the demolition of the rather odd-shaped building on the right. The shop opposite it, then the post office, has also gone. The Prince Albert (left), served in 1960 by Stroud Brewery, remains little changed. The Prince Albert first appears in the trade directory of 1914, when James Lawson was its landlord.

RODBOROUGH
The Fort 1900 45737

The entrance gates to the
Fort from Rodborough
Common are hardly ever
seen open these days. The
core of the building was
erected by George Hawker in
the 1760s. It had no water
supply until 1790. It was
rebuilt on a grander scale by
Alexander Holcombe in 1868.

THE NAILSWORTH VALLEY

Here in the Nailsworth Valley we once again see the modern road following the valley base, while earlier lanes, fringed by cottages and farms, generally meander along higher contours. The Nailsworth Valley contains many former cloth mills; easily the largest and most impressive is Dunkirk Mill, once owned by the Playne family. The mill has several surviving water-wheels. The building is now largely converted to residential use. Along the valley is Woodchester, remarkable not only for its Roman remains, but also for a side valley up which lies one of Gloucestershire's hidden treasures, the Mansion. Designed by local architect Benjamin Bucknall, the construction of this superb edifice began in the 1860s. Then, fully roofed, it was abandoned, with builders' ladders still leaning against unplastered walls and centring still in position in archways. The Mansion remains an untouched time capsule of Victorian craftsmanship.

Nailsworth was served by a railway line, linking it to Stonehouse and, via Dudbridge, to Stroud. The little steam train that ran along the side of the valley was affectionately known as the Dudbridge Donkey. The line closed to passengers in 1947 and was abandoned completely in the mid 1960s. It is now a path and cycle track.

NAILSWORTH, *General View 1890* 25172

In this early view across the town, the hill above Watledge is devoid of tree cover. The Highlands, now Beaudesert Park School, is visible on the skyline, with The Hollies below it. Immediately to the right of Nailsworth Brewery's distinctive chimney, the tower of the 'Pepperpot Church', demolished in 1898, may be glimpsed.

NAILSWORTH
1890 25171

In this early view of Nailsworth, much of the pre-Victorian nucleus of the town may be seen. In the distance, on the right, Chestnut Hill House, then the home of the Clissold family, stands out prominently. Shortwood Baptist Chapel, now Christchurch, re-sited from Shortwood village only nine years earlier, is in the centre. Much of the distant hillside has now been developed for housing.

NAILSWORTH, *1900* 45594

Here Nailsworth is seen from the 'W', the zigzag hill road linking it to Box village. By 1900 the 'Pepperpot Church' has been replaced by St George's as we know it today. Apart from fairly extensive modern building development, which has considerably altered this aspect of the town, the other point of interest in the picture lies in the tin church on the left, erected in the vicarage grounds to serve the parish while St George's was under construction. The tin church was subsequently removed.

◄ **NAILSWORTH**
Longfords Lake 1904
53117

The lake, privately owned, was justly renowned for its beauty, especially in autumn. Three boathouses existed along its banks, of which the chalet type, seen here, is the most interesting example. Longfords Lake was noted during Victorian times for its trout fishing, but unfortunately roach were introduced and pike had then to be brought in to control them, which did little for the trout fishing.

◀ **NAILSWORTH**
1900 45595

Viewed from Watledge, the Railway Hotel is shown clearly in the centre of the picture, with C W Jones' coal office behind the chimney to the right. Beyond the hotel building is Day's Mill, with St George's church a little back to the left. The cottage in the foreground shows an unusual method of loft ventilation.

▲ **NAILSWORTH,** *Longfords Lake 1910* 62688

Longfords Lake was created in 1806 as a reservoir to feed the large nearby cloth mill run by the Playne family. Originally 15 acres in extent, it is now much silted up. The bill for the original construction of the dam was £945.

◀ **HORSLEY**
1907 53127

Horsley is one of the ancient parishes from which Nailsworth was formed in the 1890s, the others being Avening and Minchinhampton. Horsley is approached from the north by the main road from Nailsworth, middle right, and by a steep lane leading from the attractive hamlet of Washpool, bottom right, where the remains of the sheep-dipping tank, which gave it its name, may still be seen.

▼ **WOODCHESTER,** *The Valley 1910* 62686

Here again we see a road that is now overhung with mature trees and was formerly clear of undergrowth. The hill leads from the Bear Hotel down to the A46 and on to North Woodchester, visible in the distance. Out of sight on the far hill to the right lie the remains of a 66-roomed Roman villa, with a superb, though incomplete, Orpheus mosaic.

► **WOODCHESTER**
1910 62684

On the left is Woodchester's Dominican priory. To the right lies the Franciscan nunnery of the Poor Clares. Hidden up the distant valley on the left is the celebrated Woodchester Mansion.

◀ **WOODCHESTER**
*The Monastery
and the Roman
Catholic Church
1900* 45592

The monastery was
established in 1853 by
William Leigh of
Woodchester Park.
Leigh was responsible
for erecting several
other Catholic
buildings in the area,
such as the church at
Nympsfield. The
monastery's domestic
structures were
designed by the
architect Charles
Hanson, and were
taken down in 1970.
The church survives.

▶ **WOODCHESTER**
The Village 1890 25173

In the foreground is the bridge
carrying the present A46 over
the Stonehouse to Nailsworth
Railway, which opened in 1867.
The Baptist chapel is near the
top of the lane rising from
Frogmarsh. Far right is the
Anglican church. Its predecessor
stood further north, at the site
of the Roman villa.

THROUGH THE STONEHOUSE VALLEY

From Stroud, the Stonehouse Valley extends west, becoming broader as it is absorbed into the Severn Valley. At its edges are various elevated viewpoints, such as Selsley Hill, Frocester Hill and Randwick, in addition to the isolated summit of Doverow Hill, close to Stonehouse itself.

The most important of the former cloth mills in the Stonehouse Valley is Ebley Mill, now extensively restored and functioning as the headquarters building for Stroud District Council. Ebley Mill was erected by the Marling family, and so were Stanley Park, their principal residence, and Selsley church, both of which overlook it. An industrial building of outstanding significance within the valley is the early 19th-century Stanley Mill, with its pioneering iron frame construction.

In the mid 18th century an attempt at making navigable the River Frome, which meanders gently through the valley, was followed by the cutting of the Stroudwater Canal, which opened for trade in 1779.

The fertility of the valley was recognised in Roman times, and potsherds in freshly ploughed fields mark the sites of several villas, the most notable of which are those at Frocester.

STROUD, *Cainscross 1925* 77567

This part of Cainscross is much altered today. All the shops and houses on the left were demolished when Tricorn House was built. In front of the tea rooms is a distinctive mile-post with a sundial top (left). It was later re-sited, but then damaged. Bridge Street, ahead, is now a cul-de-sac. The toll-house on the right has recently been restored.

STROUD
Cainscross looking towards Ebley 1925
77565

The large, distinctive shop premises on the left contain the headquarters of the Cainscross and Ebley Co-operative Society; when this picture was taken, it had recently celebrated its Diamond Jubilee. On the right is the White Horse Inn, a long-established public house where property auctions were held in the early 19th century.

▼ **SELSLEY**, *View from the Hill 1910* 62672

Selsley was, until 1863, a part of Kings Stanley ecclesiastical parish. The church's design is based on one at Marlengo in the Tyrol, and has important glass from the workshops of William Morris. It was built by Sir Samuel Marling, whose woollen cloth mill is visible in the valley beyond. The monument to the left of the church came from the 1851 Great Exhibition. The main point of interest in the picture, however, lies in the distance, where much recent building development has radically altered the landscape.

▶ **STONEHOUSE**
From Doverow Hill c1950 S265006

Most of the commercial centre of present-day Stonehouse dates back no further than the 19th century, when the Great Western Railway line from Swindon to Cheltenham was put through. Its station, now much reduced in size, is on the left of the picture. However, along the main street, and elsewhere in Stonehouse, some interesting early buildings do still survive and are worth searching out.

◄ **STONEHOUSE**
High Street c1955
S265012

This shot of the High Street indeed proves the point that, among Stonehouse's predominantly Victorian buildings, a few much earlier houses still remain: the half-timbered cottage is currently the Tudor Tandoori. Gardiner's Garage has been replaced by a Co-operative Society store. The bread shop on the far right, founded in 1790, is still a baker's, and Gillo's remains a butcher's, now run as Broomhall's.

► **STONEHOUSE**
The Green c1955
S265013

Over the last half century the Green has altered very little. The pump and war memorial remain unchanged, although the Victorian double-gabled house beyond has lost its original porch, and the windows of the Globe Inn have been altered. The pub has also lost its tall chimney.

STONEHOUSE
High Street c1960
S265023

Of the shops on the right, the Midland Bank is now, of course, HSBC. The well-stocked newsagent (right) has become a Sue Ryder shop, and Brinkworth's hardware store beyond it has been replaced by a building society. The mature cedar tree has gone, along with the Congregational chapel in whose grounds it stood. Behind the chapel site, back from the road, its gravestones have been preserved.

STONEHOUSE
Quietways c1960
S265045

The shops in Elm Road are structurally much the same today, although they have changed ownership. For example, Walter's bakery is now a pet shop. St Cyr's Parish Hall is in the distance. Today, the new primary school buildings are beyond it. The large, stone building down Quietways, on the right, was the vicarage.

FROCESTER
George Hotel and Memorial c1955
F147005

As its name suggests, Frocester was occupied in Roman times. A villa, explored some forty years ago, exists beneath the now demolished St Peter's church. A second villa, meticulously excavated, lies in fields near Frocester's celebrated tithe barn. The village pub, The George, at one time renamed The Royal Gloucestershire Hussar, has now happily reverted to its former title.

FROCESTER, *The Village from Frocester Hill c1960* F147003

The second Roman villa referred to earlier lies beneath the furthermost of the large fields in the foreground, known as Great Stanborough. In the far distance, across the Severn, is May Hill, with its distinctive pine copse. Today, the M5 bisects the agricultural land in the middle distance. Several of the oaks have succumbed to age or disease: the one on the left lies shattered in pieces.

HARESFIELD, *The Holy Well 1914* 66568

Situated on the Cotswold Way, near the lane from Harescombe to Edge, is the Holy Well, erected in 1870 in local limestone. It has unusual floral finials. Inside the little building a carved plaque contains the following lines:

Deo Gratias

Whoe'r the Bucketfull upwindeth

Let him bless God who Water findeth,

Yet Water here but small availeth:

Go seek that Well which never faileth.

John c4 v14

79

THE PAINSWICK VALLEY AND BEYOND

Here, once again, the modern road to Painswick follows a route nearer to the valley bottom, while the old route, via Wick Street, rises quickly and meanders along the hillside at a higher level, passing some fine examples of Cotswold stone houses. Wick Street is, incidentally, a prehistoric route – the Jurassic Way, leading down from the Midlands. Painswick itself is a delight, with its narrow streets, picturesque corners and a gravestone collection of national importance. Local stone predominates throughout the town, and only the most assiduous searcher might discover the odd red brick outhouse or wall.

Beyond Painswick is the Beacon, with its well-preserved prehistoric earthworks and spectacular views across the Severn Valley to the Malvern Hills and further to Wales and the Black Mountains. Above Painswick, up side valleys, lie beautiful villages such as Sheepscombe and Cranham, the hilltops above them heavily wooded with beech, the predominant tree in the upland areas of the Stroud district.

Painswick was, until the early 19th century, an extensive parish, from which several other parishes were formed. Prinknash Park, where the abbey now is, was historically an extra-parochial area.

PAINSWICK, *1901* 47362

Full of architectural gems and surprises, Painswick has been called the 'Queen of the Cotswolds'. Whether seen, as here, in the distance from the south, or viewed from close to, it is not hard to see why this lovely old Cotswold town was so titled.

PAINSWICK
The Church 1890
25181

Painswick churchyard is celebrated both for its yew trees and also for its unique collection of table tombs and other funerary monuments, including, incidentally, a pyramid! Each autumn the 'clipping' ceremony takes place, in which, during a special service, a large circle of parishioners, including many children, surround the church, holding hands, singing and moving in and out in time to a traditional hymn.

PAINSWICK, *Bisley Street c1960* P3027

On the left and in the distance are notable examples of early local buildings. The large house on the extreme left, until recently the National Trust Bookshop, is especially fine. It may date from medieval times. It was rebuilt around 1600 and restored in 1942.

SHEEPSCOMBE
1910 62704

The attractive village of Sheepscombe was formerly part of the large, ancient parish of Painswick. Its church was built in 1820 and was given its own ecclesiastical district in 1844. The tower is of a distinctive design. Quarry workings are visible on the distant slope.

CRANHAM
Prinkash Abbey,
St Peter's Grange c1960
C179035

Medieval in origin, this building had by 1526 been enlarged into a manor house for the Abbots of Gloucester. In 1535 Henry VIII and Anne Boleyn hunted in Prinknash Park. After the Dissolution the estate passed through the hands of several families, such as the Bridges and Bridgemans. In 1924 Thomas Dyer Edwardes invited Benedictine monks from Caldey Island to establish a foundation at Prinknash.

CRANHAM, *Prinkash Abbey, The Laity Chapel c1960* C179033

The monks needed to extend and develop the old buildings at Prinknash. Soon after their arrival in 1928 the transept shown here was added to the chapel. W Heath Robinson, whose son was a monk at the abbey, painted a cartoon of the restoration work. In 1939, however, the foundation stone of a new monastery across the valley was laid, although the monks also continued to occupy the Old Grange. The crypt of the new abbey was consecrated in 1972. Incense-making has taken place at Prinknash for many years, and a Bird Park helps to attract visitors. The celebrated Prinknash Pottery has recently closed, sad to say.

THE SLAD VALLEY

The Slad Valley is the smallest and least developed of the five that meet at Stroud. Once the Victorian and 20th-century housing at Uplands has been left behind, the Slad Valley soon takes on a rural appearance. To admire it at its best there is no better vantage point than Swifts Hill, with its glorious, westward views towards Stroud. Sunsets here are particularly impressive.

There were several woollen cloth mills in the Slad Valley, although some disappeared at an early period. Easily the largest was Vatch Mill, demolished at the end of the 19th century.

There is no part of the Stroud area so well known nationally – even internationally – as the Slad Valley. The reason is, of course, Laurie Lee's celebrated childhood autobiography, *Cider with Rosie*, published in the 1950s. This affectionate portrait of a small community witnessing the end of a rural way of life stretching back largely unchanged for centuries is unparalleled in English literature.

From Slad village, beyond Bulls Cross in quiet corners of side valleys, are cottages and farms as isolated and picturesque as any to be found in the Stroud district.

SLAD, *Trillgate Farm 1910* 62705

Near Bull's Cross - named after an old inn - is Trillgate Farm. It lies in an idyllic setting. The building is now substantially altered by a wing added on the left. Place names in the valleys near Trillgate are intriguing: Piedmont, Dillay, Sydenham's, The Scrubs and Bunnage.

SLAD
The Village 1910
62707

Slad church was built in 1834, and is as easily recognisable as the one at Sheepscombe. Laurie Lee, who died in 1997, is buried beneath a yew tree in the village graveyard. Immediately to the left of the church is the Woolpack Inn.

SLAD, *Steanbridge Lane 1910* 62706

The L-shaped building in the foreground, with its blocked windows, was known as The Old House. Down the lane which passes behind it and leads to the right is the pond in which, in *Cider with Rosie,* the body of the unfortunate Miss Flynn was discovered floating. Steanbridge House, where Laurie Lee's Squire Jones lived, is approached by way of this lane.

INDEX

NAMES OF SUBSCRIBERS

Emma Adamson

Jo Adamson

Paul Adamson

Oscar Adamson

Rupert Adamson

Del and Sandra Bevan

Stephen Bingle, Stroud

L. J. K. Blacktin

Lauren Brown

Mark Brown

Phillipa Brown

D. W. J. Burford

E. M. Burford

M. S. Burford

Ron Burge, Stroud

Mr & Mrs G. A. Cleaveley

Ian Cleaveley

A. J. Cole, Bristol

Sue Collins, Ebley

Will Dangerfield

Matthew C. G. Dyer, Stroud

Richard & Barbara Ford

Emma Funnell

Jacqueline Funnell

Peter Funnell

Mr & Mrs R. D. Funnell

David & Thelma Greening

Richard Harding

Peter Hocking, Rodborough

Chris Hodgson

Jane Hodgson

Pauline Hooley

Mrs W. Hosier, Stroud

Molly Hoy

Anthlony F. Hudson, Stroud

Barbara Humphries

Richard Humphries

Cedric John

Christine John

Emma John

Oliver Jordan

Barbara Kilmister

George Kilmister

Tina Kilmister

Connor Kinnear

Finn Kinnear

Zak Kinnear

Darren Long

Johanna Long

Mary Long

Mr E. J. Major, Stroud

Amy Mason

Gordon Mills, Cashes Green

Jane Mooney

Pat Mooney

Ian Prout

Val Prout

Kirsty Rattcliffe

Miles Rattcliffe

Richard Rattcliffe

Jane Read

Steve Read

G. Richards, Stroud

Bill Roberts (Pops)

John. E. Rogers, Ruscombe

Brian Roseblade

Kay Roseblade

Richard Small

Stephanie Small

Rod, Ben & Charlie Smith of Stroud

Dawn Stevens

Debbie Stevens

Robert Stevens

Roger Stevens

Caitlin Taylor

Jennifer Taylor

Julia Taylor

Leonard Taylor

Oliver Taylor

Samuel Taylor

Mr & Mrs Thornhill, Stroud

John Thwaite

Melissa Thwaite

Peter A. W. Tims, Stroud

Erica Ward

Hannah Weaver

Katherine Weaver

Alan Keith Webb

Simon Webb

Jonathan Wells

Clive Wright, Stroud

Derek Yorke

FRITH PRODUCTS & SERVICES

Francis Frith would doubtless be pleased to know that the pioneering publishing venture he started in 1860 still continues today. Over a hundred and forty years later, The Francis Frith Collection continues in the same innovative tradition and is now one of the foremost publishers of vintage photographs in the world. Some of the current activities include:

Interior Decoration

Today Frith's photographs can be seen framed and as giant wall murals in thousands of pubs, restaurants, hotels, banks, retail stores and other public buildings throughout the country. In every case they enhance the unique local atmosphere of the places they depict and provide reminders of gentler days in an increasingly busy and frenetic world.

Product Promotions

Frith products are used by many major companies to promote the sales of their own products or to reinforce their own history and heritage. Frith promotions have been used by Hovis bread, Courage beers, Scots Porage Oats, Colman's mustard, Cadbury's foods, Mellow Birds coffee, Dunhill pipe tobacco, Guinness, and Bulmer's Cider.

Genealogy and Family History

As the interest in family history and roots grows world-wide, more and more people are turning to Frith's photographs of Great Britain for images of the towns, villages and streets where their ancestors lived; and, of course, photographs of the churches and chapels where their ancestors were christened, married and buried are an essential part of every genealogy tree and family album.

Frith Products

All Frith photographs are available Framed or just as Mounted Prints and Posters (size 23 x 16 inches). These may be ordered from the address below. From time to time other products - Address Books, Calendars, Table Mats, etc - are available.

The Internet

Already fifty thousand Frith photographs can be viewed and purchased on the internet through the Frith websites and a myriad of partner sites.

For more detailed information on Frith companies and products, look at these sites:

www.francisfrith.co.uk
www.francisfrith.com
(for North American visitors)

See the complete list of Frith Books at:

www.francisfrith.co.uk

This web site is regularly updated with the latest list of publications from the Frith Book Company. If you wish to buy books relating to another part of the country that your local bookshop does not stock, you may purchase on-line.

For further information, trade, or author enquiries please contact us at the address below:
The Francis Frith Collection, Frith's Barn, Teffont, Salisbury, Wiltshire, England SP3 5QP.
Tel: +44 (0) 1722 716 376 Fax: +44 (0) 1722 716 881   Email: sales@francisfrith.co.uk

See Frith books on the internet at www.francisfrith.co.uk

FREE MOUNTED PRINT

Mounted Print
Overall size 14 x 11 inches

Fill in and cut out this voucher and return
it with your remittance for £2.25 (to cover postage and handling). Offer valid for delivery to UK addresses only.

Choose any photograph included in this book.
Your SEPIA print will be A4 in size. It will be mounted in a cream mount with a burgundy rule line (overall size 14 x 11 inches).

**Order additional Mounted Prints
at HALF PRICE (only £7.49 each*)**
If you would like to order more Frith prints from this book, possibly as gifts for friends and family, you can buy them at half price (with no additional postage and handling costs).

Have your Mounted Prints framed
For an extra £14.95 per print* you can have your mounted print(s) framed in an elegant polished wood and gilt moulding, overall size 16 x 13 inches (no additional postage and handling required).

---

* IMPORTANT!

These special prices are only available if you order at the same time as you order your free mounted print. You must use the ORIGINAL VOUCHER on this page (no copies permitted). We can only despatch to one address.

Send completed Voucher form to:
The Francis Frith Collection, Frith's Barn, Teffont, Salisbury, Wiltshire SP3 5QP

CHOOSE ANY IMAGE FROM THIS BOOK

Voucher for **FREE** *and Reduced Price Frith Prints*

Please do not photocopy this voucher. Only the original is valid, so please fill it in, cut it out and return it to us with your order.

Picture ref no	Page no	Qty	Mounted @ £7.49	Framed + £14.95	Total Cost
		1	Free of charge*	£	£
			£7.49	£	£
			£7.49	£	£
			£7.49	£	£
			£7.49	£	£
			£7.49	£	£
Please allow 28 days for delivery			* Post & handling (UK)		£2.25
			Total Order Cost		£

Title of this book . . . .

I enclose a cheque/postal order for £ . . . .
made payable to 'The Francis Frith Collection'

OR please debit my Mastercard / Visa / Switch / Amex card
(credit cards please on all overseas orders), details below

Card Number

Issue No (Switch only)   Valid from (Amex/Switch)

Expires   Signature

Name Mr/Mrs/Ms . . . .
Address . . . .
. . . .
. . . .
. . . . Postcode . . . .
Daytime Tel No . . . .
Email . . . .

Valid to 31/12/05

Free Print – see overleaf

Would you like to find out more about Francis Frith?

We have recently recruited some entertaining speakers who are happy to visit local groups, clubs and societies to give an illustrated talk documenting Frith's travels and photographs. If you are a member of such a group and are interested in hosting a presentation, we would love to hear from you.

Our speakers bring with them a small selection of our local town and county books, together with sample prints. They are happy to take orders. A small proportion of the order value is donated to the group who have hosted the presentation. The talks are therefore an excellent way of fundraising for small groups and societies.

Can you help us with information about any of the Frith photographs in this book?

We are gradually compiling an historical record for each of the photographs in the Frith archive. It is always fascinating to find out the names of the people shown in the pictures, as well as insights into the shops, buildings and other features depicted.

If you recognize anyone in the photographs in this book, or if you have information not already included in the author's caption, do let us know. We would love to hear from you, and will try to publish it in future books or articles.

Our production team

Frith books are produced by a small dedicated team at offices in the converted Grade II listed 18th-century barn at Teffont near Salisbury, illustrated above. Most have worked with the Frith Collection for many years. All have in common one quality: they have a passion for the Frith Collection. The team is constantly expanding, but currently includes:

Jason Buck, John Buck, Douglas Mitchell-Burns, Ruth Butler, Heather Crisp, Isobel Hall, Julian Hight, Peter Horne, James Kinnear, Karen Kinnear, Tina Leary, David Marsh, Sue Molloy, Kate Rotondetto, Dean Scource, Eliza Sackett, Terence Sackett, Sandra Sampson, Adrian Sanders, Sandra Sanger, Julia Skinner, Lewis Taylor, Shelley Tolcher and Lorraine Tuck.